How To Crochet Blanket

Step By Step Guide To Crochet Blanket For Beginners

Copyright © 2020

All rights reserved.

DEDICATION

The author and publisher have provided this e-book to you for your personal use only. You may not make this e-book publicly available in any way. Copyright infringement is against the law. If you believe the copy of this e-book you are reading infringes on the author's copyright, please notify the publisher at: https://us.macmillan.com/piracy

Contents

Crochet a Baby Blanket..1
Striped Lace Baby Blanket...................................8
Cheerful Ripple Crochet Blanket......................17
Crochet Doll Blanket...23
The Granny Stripe Blanket................................29
Twinkling Stars Blanket.....................................36

Crochet a Baby Blanket

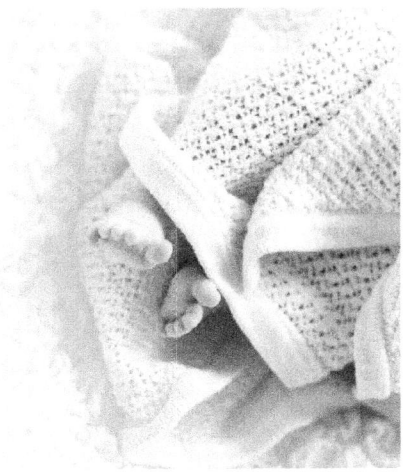

Working Time: 24 hrs

Total Time: 24 hrs

Yield: 1 baby blanket

Skill Level: Beginner

When you first learn how to crochet a blanket, you want one that is quick and easy so you don't have to wait for weeks to see the results of your efforts. As far as crochet baby blankets go, this one is a fast, easy crochet project. It uses only two basic crochet stitches: single crochet and chain stitch. And using a larger-than-usual hook size gives added drape to the blanket and helps the work to go a little faster than it would otherwise.

This pattern is easy enough for beginners, but this is also a good pattern for crocheters of all skill levels who want a quick and easy project to work on. This is a good crochet pattern for meditative crochet since it has an easy repeat and uses only basic crochet stitches. It is the type of easy crochet baby blanket that you can work on when waiting in lines, sitting in the car, or watching television.

What You'll Need

Equipment / Tools

Crochet hook

Tapestry needle

Stitch marker

Materials

Bernat Softee baby yarn

Instructions

Yarn Information

The recommended yarn for this project is Bernat Softee baby yarn. The weight is "light worsted," "DK," or "Double Knitting." This is important to know in case you want to select a different yarn to substitute; look for the same weight if you aim to create a blanket with the same drape. That said, you can use any yarn weight and a corresponding hook size to create an easy crochet baby blanket using this pattern.

Blanket Sizes: Preemie, Newborn, Toddler

This crochet baby blanket pattern includes instructions for three sizes: preemie, newborn, and toddler. Instructions list the smallest size first with changes for the larger sizes noted in parentheses.

The measurements below don't include any edging; if you wish to add a baby blanket edging, your finished blanket will be a little bit bigger.

Preemie: The smallest blanket measures about 26 inches wide by 34 inches long. If you crochet your blanket using Bernat Softee, you will need two to three 5-oz skeins of yarn to complete this project, depending on how tight you crochet. As far as yardage goes, you'll need about 724 yards/662 meters for the blanket itself, plus a bit more for your gauge swatch.

Newborn/receiving blanket: The mid-sized blanket is 30 inches square. You can make it a little bit longer if you prefer a more rectangular shape for the blanket. If so, aim for 30" x 34". You will need two to three of the 5-oz balls of Bernat Softee for this size, depending on how tight you crochet.

Toddler: The largest of the blankets measures 36 inches by 44 inches. You will need four 5-oz balls of Bernat Softee to crochet this size.

Abbreviations Used in This Pattern

ch = chain

ch-1 sp = chain-1 space, the space formed when you crochet a chain stitch in the previous row

rep = repeat

sc = single crochet

st = stitch

Gauge

Stitch gauge: 4 stitches = 1 inch when crocheting the stitch pattern as instructed below.

Row gauge: The row gauge is not important for this pattern.

Crochet a Gauge Swatch

To check your gauge, crochet a gauge swatch. Form a starting chain of 25 stitches and crochet using the blanket pattern instructions until your piece is square. End off. Measure your swatch to see how many stitches per inch you are crocheting. Compare your gauge against that recommended in the pattern (above). If you are crocheting fewer stitches per inch than recommended, try again with a smaller crochet hook. If you are crocheting more stitches per inch, try again with a larger hook.

The swatching process is necessary because you want your baby blanket to be a useable size. If your gauge is different, your baby blanket could finish at the wrong size or you may run out of yarn before finishing the blanket.

Design Notes

The pattern directions instruct you to crochet into the ch-1 spaces. If you have difficulty finding these—sometimes they seem to vanish—carefully poke your finger at the row of stitches from back to front. Your hands will feel the gap even if your eyes don't spot it at first.

How to Crochet a Baby Blanket

Begin Row One

Ch 105 (121, 145). Remember, the instructions are for the small size (with the medium, large in the parenthesis).

Place a stitch marker in the first ch from your hook. Sc in 3rd ch from hook. [ch 1, skip next ch, sc in next ch.] Rep across the entire row. ch 1, turn.

Start on Row Two

[sc in the next ch-1 sp, ch 1.] Rep the sequence in brackets across the rest of the row. At the end of the row, work a sc st into the st where you placed the marker; you can remove the marker before working the stitch. ch 1, turn.

Continue Rows Three and Up

The rest of the rows are all exactly the same as row 2, with one minor difference: at the end of the row, work your last sc st into the turning chain of the previous row. Rep this row until the baby blanket reaches your desired length.

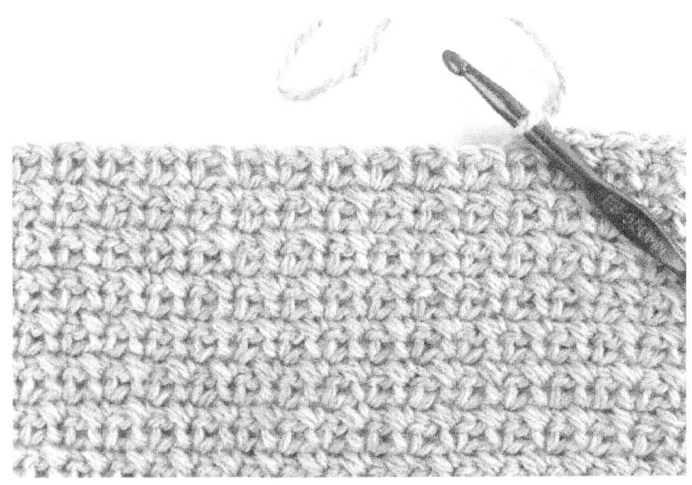

Tip

When you need to change to a new ball of yarn, use the same technique as you would for changing colors.

Finish Off Your Blanket

When the baby blanket is the length that you want, cut the yarn, leaving at least six inches of extra yarn. Thread the tapestry needle with the yarn end and use the needle to weave the loose end of the yarn into the blanket. Repeat with any other loose ends you may have hanging from the blanket (which occur when you switch from one ball of yarn to the next).

This crochet pattern works fine without any additional edging, but you can add an edging if you want to. There are many baby blanket edgings to choose from. A simple single crochet stitch around the entire edge of the blanket is an easy choice that goes well with the single crochet design in this pattern.

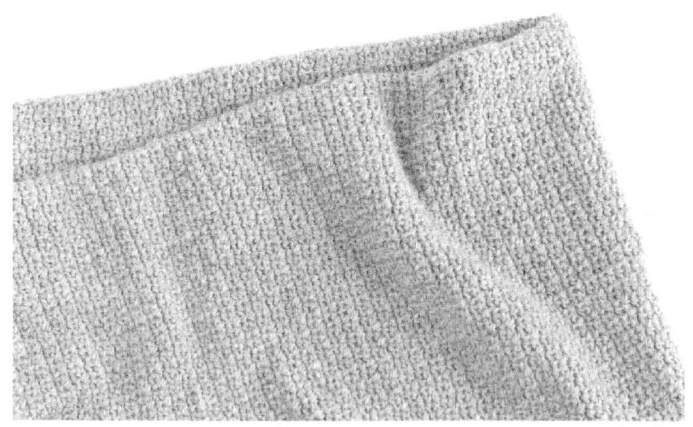

Striped Lace Baby Blanket

Skill Level: Intermediate

This free crochet edging pattern uses the V-stitch in combination with picots to create a unique border. It works exceptionally well around openwork designs, including those that make use of V-stitches, but is a versatile border for everything from crochet blankets to cardigans. This crochet edging is a wide border, and you'll learn here how to work it around all four sides of a square or rectangular project. Use it on a single edge to enhance a design such as a shawl or a pillowcase.

Abbreviations

ch = chain

ch # = chain # stitches, where # is the specified number of stitches

ch-# sp = chain-# space; the space formed by the specified number of chain stitches in the previous row/rnd

dc = double crochet

rep = repeat

sc = single crochet

sl = slip

sp = space

st(s) = stitch(es)

v-st = v-stitch; worked as (dc, ch 1, dc) in same sp or st

( ) = repeat instructions within ( ) as directed; repeats are often in same stitch or space

Notes

You may adjust your yarn weight and crochet hook as needed when adding this border to different types of projects. For a consistent look it is best to match the yarn used in the project.

What You'll Need

Equipment / Tools

US I/9 (5.5 mm) crochet hook

Yarn or tapestry needle

Materials

Swatch to edge, any stitch pattern

DK or worsted weight yarn for edging

Instructions

Begin With Single Crochet

With your edging yarn, make a slip knot and place it on your hook. Join the yarn to the work with a single crochet stitch in a corner at the right end of the top or bottom of the project.

Side: work one sc in each st to the last st.

Turn corner: sc in last st of edge, ch 2, turn the work 90 degrees, sc in same space as last sc.

Single Crochet Edging

Single Crochet Remaining Sides

Work single crochet down next side, turn corner; work sc across next side, turn corner; work sc up final side, back to where you started.

At the first corner, ch 2 and sl st to first sc to join.

Tip

Check the gauge of your single crochet so that the number of stitches you make in your side edges is appropriate for its height in inches.

Single Crochet Border

Begin V-Stitch

Remember a V-stitch is created by working (dc, ch 1, dc) in the same space or stitch.

Begin with ch 3, sk 1 sc.

Side: *v-st in next sc, skip 2 sts; rep from * to the corner.

Corner: (v-st, ch 2, v-st) in same ch-2 sp.

Rep Side and Corner twice more, then Side once.

Corner Join: work v-st in ch-2 sp, ch 2; create final v-st from ch 3 at beg of round: dc in base of the chain, ch1, join to top of ch 3 with sl st.

Work second round of V-stitch in next step if desired, or go to Picot step.

V-Stitch Border Free Crochet Pattern

Second V-Stitch Round (Optional)
Sl st in center of first v-st.

Begin with ch 4 (counts as 1 dc, ch 1), dc in same sp to complete v-st,

Side: *v-st in ch-1 sp of next v-st; rep from * to the corner.

Corner: work v-st in ch-2 corner sp.

Rep Side and Corner twice more, then Side once.

Corner V-St Join: use sl st to join to 3rd ch of first ch 4.

Tip

If you wanted to do something a little bit different with this round, try crochet v-stitch shells instead of classic v-stitches.

Picot Round

A round of picots finished the crochet border pattern. There will be one picot stitch worked into each V-stitch; corner stitches are worked the same was as every other V-stitch.

Work a sl st in ch-1 space in the center of next v-st, sc in center of same st, ch 3, sl st in 3rd ch from hook, sc in v-st—first picot complete.

Picot rnd: *sl st in sp between v-sts, (sc, ch 3, sl st in 3rd ch from hook, sc) in ch-1 sp; rep from * around piece, sl st to join after last corner.

Finishing

Fasten off. Use a yarn or tapestry needle to weave in ends.

Cheerful Ripple Crochet Blanket

The pattern is easy peasy, so I thought I'd share it. It's just sets of 14 treble stitches, plus three turning chains.

I used Robin Double Knit* acrylic 100g (300m 328yds) for a blanket/throw 46 x 52 inches or 117x133 cm - any similar DK, light worsted weight or 8 ply, depending which continent you're on - would do.

50g ball each of 11 colours of your choice, mine were:

Fondant

Pale Rose (looks more lavender in the photos)

Cordial

Apple

Acid yellow

Lemon

Madonna

Turquoise

Jade

Red

Peach

Size 5mm H/8 Hook

To decide on my colour scheme, I cut a small piece of each colour yarn and play about until I'm happy with the arrangement and the order. Then I tape it onto a piece of white card to keep as a reminder, like a swatch.

If you use US terms UK treble is a double crochet so just substitute dc.

Tr3tog - * yoh, insert hook into the next st, yoh, pull through, yoh, pull through first 2 loops, rep from * twice, yoh, draw through all 4 loops on hook

Chain 14 and repeat until you get your desired width. Then add three more stitches.

Row 1

Skip the first 2 ch (this counts as 1 tr),

2 tr into next ch,

*1tr into next 3 ch

then using the next 3 stitches tr3tog

again, using the next 3 stitches tr3tog

1 tr into next 3 chain

3 tr into next 2 chain*

Repeat from * to * all the way to the end of the row and make sure you end with 3tr.

Row 2

Chain 3 (counts as 1 tr)

2 tr into first stitch

* 1tr into next 3 stitches

then using the next 3 stitches tr3tog

again, using the next 3 stitches tr3tog 1 tr into next 3 stitches

3tr int next 2 chain*

Repeat from * to * all the way to the end of the row and end with 3tr.

Repeat Row 2 pattern twice, then fasten off and join in a new colour

Do this twice more, joining a new colour at the end of every second row.

On Row 9 do only one row before changing colour.

You can see where I've done this on the piccie below) So every 9th row has only one 'ripple' instead of 2. Repeat from the beginning until you have your desired length.

I decided on a simple plain edging in red and blue to 'frame' the ripples. Crochet three rounds in dc (US sc), at each corner crochet 4 dc into the corner stitch to 'make' your corner. The last two rounds are in htr, again you make 4 stitches into each corner stitch. That's it, I hope it makes sense, but I'm sure someone will tell me if it doesn't!

Crochet blankets must, of course, meet my teddy test. Himself's gorgeous Blue Ted (aged 50) and my adorable Cuddles (a mere babe at 46) think it's great! You may wonder why they are both in such immaculate condition....

Well, I asked for a new teddy when I was 7 and everyone said I was too old, except my lovely Auntie Mary (who also started me embroidering). She bought Cuddles for my birthday and I treated him like a mascot rather than a toy. (At one stage he did have an 'Osmonds' top which I embroidered, and briefly one for the Bay City Rollers and a tartan scarf, but - hey- I was very young!) He's beautiful and still has his growl.

Blue Ted's story is very sad. Adored by his little owner and taken everywhere (and yes, I mean everywhere) he dropped into the potty one day- while it was being used. Despite being washed and cleaned thoroughly, he was cast aside by his owner - (how sad to be so fickle at such a young age!). I am just very glad he was kept. He is a Wendy Boston bear, an iconic British 1950's and 60's design - and extremely cute

You'll be happy to hear Blue Ted got over his traumatic experience and has now been fully rehabilitated, living happily in the hug with the other bears. Keep snug!

Crochet Doll Blanket

Making crochet doll clothes and accessories is a lot of fun because it allows you to make a wide variety of items in miniature versions. It's a great way to practice stitches and get familiar with techniques on small projects. You can always take what you learn and implement it to full size if you love the pattern, or you can just make lots of beautiful things for a doll collection.

This crochet doll blanket is designed to cover an 18"

doll including the American Girl dolls. This is a simple crochet blanket pattern that uses v-stitches for detail. If you've never worked with crochet v-stitch before, then this blanket provides a great opportunity for practice. If it's a stitch that you love, you'll find this to be a meditative project.

At the end of the instructions, you'll find information about how to adapt this pattern to make things other than the crochet doll blanket. This 18.5" v-stitch crochet square can be turned into a larger blanket, a cowl, a placemat, and more. You'll be surprised by what you can do with this one simple pattern.

Crochet Doll Blanket Details

There are a few things that you might want to know before you begin working on this free crochet doll blanket pattern.

Materials

6 ounces worsted weight yarn, any color

Size G crochet hook

Large eye tapestry needle for weaving in ends

Finished size:

18 1/2 inches x 18 1/2 inches

Gauge

1 V-Stitch plus 1 double crochet = 1 inch

2 double crochet rows = 1 inch

Stitches Used

The following crochet stitches and abbreviations are used in the project. These are US crochet terms.

ch - chain

ch-1 sp - chain 1 space

sc - single crochet

dc - double crochet

v-stitch: double crochet in next single crochet, chain 1, double crochet in same single crochet

Crochet Doll Blanket Pattern

Before you begin, let's give you a lay of the land so that you know what you are going to be doing.

Each row of this crochet blanket begins and ends with 3 double crochet stitches. In between, you will have v-stitches separated by double crochet stitches.

You will always crochet v's into v's (working into the chain space of the v below) and crochet the stand-alone double crochet stitches (which are in between the v's) into the double crochet stitches from the row below. The pattern begins and ends with a row of single crochet stitches to create a border for the blanket.

Okay, now here is how to do it:

Starting chain: Chain 70.

Row 1: Single crochet in 2nd chain from hook, single crochet in each chain across. (Total = 69 single crochet)

Row 2: chain 3 (counts as first double crochet), double crochet in each of next 2 single crochet, * skip next single crochet, v-stitch, skip next single crochet, double crochet in next single crochet *, repeat from * to * 14 more times, skip next single crochet, v-stitch, skip next single crochet, double crochet in last 3 single crochet.

Row 3: chain 3 (counts as 1st double crochet), double crochet in next 2 double crochet, * v-stitch in chain 1 space, double crochet in next double crochet*, repeat from * to * 14 more times, v-stitch in chain 1 space, double crochet in last 3 double crochet.

Rows 4 - 36: Repeat row 3.

Row 37: chain 1, sc in first 4 dc, * sc in chain 1 space, sc in next 3 dc*, repeat from * to * across row, sc in last dc.

End off, leaving a length of yarn about 6 inches long. Weave in ends, using a large-eye yarn needle.

Other Ways to Use This Crochet Pattern

This crochet pattern is designed like a doll blanket. However, it is a terrific crochet square pattern that could also be used for a variety of other projects. In its current size, this crochet pattern also works as:

Placemat/table setting

Square dishtowel; you could also make fewer rows (less of the "repeat Row 3") for a rectangular dishtowel

A crochet cowl pattern; make two of them, place

back to back, join together on both side seams

A crochet scarf pattern; make three or four of them (depending on the length that you want) and join them together vertically

A large blanket square; make nine of them and join together (3x3) for a great crochet blanket.

Once you have any kind of crochet square pattern, you can make all different types of things that are based on the design of the square. This crochet pattern, where V-stitches are bordered by single crochet, is a terrific design that is easy even for beginner crafters, so it is a good one to keep in your library for when you want to design something based on the square.

You can make this square smaller or larger by changing your choice of hook and yarn. Work it with a lightweight yarn and a steel thread crochet hook for small projects. Work it with bulky yarn and a size K or larger hook to make something much bigger. Play around with all of the options; this is a versatile crochet square pattern that works for many more things than just the beautiful crochet doll blanket it makes so well.

The Granny Stripe Blanket

Who doesn't love a granny stripe? The granny stripe blanket is in my opinion, the most quintessential crochet blanket of them all... They have been around for decades and the basic pattern is so easy to master. You only need to know a few basic stitches and in no time at all, you can create a gorgeous, squishy, stripy, colourful blanket, perfect for snuggles on the sofa.

US terms are used throughout.

Abbreviations

sc Single crochet

dc Double crochet

sl st Slip stitch

ch Chain

sp Space

sk skip

Notes: You can use any yarn weight you like with this stitch, just use the hook size recommended on your yarn ball band.

Foundation Chain   a multiple of 3 + 1 (keep chaining until you reach the required width of your blanket).

Row 1 dc in the 4th chain from hook, *sk 2 chains, 3 dc in the next chain* repeat from * to * until the last 3 chains, sk 2 chains and 2 dc in the last chain. Turn. We will now be working in the spaces between each group of stitches

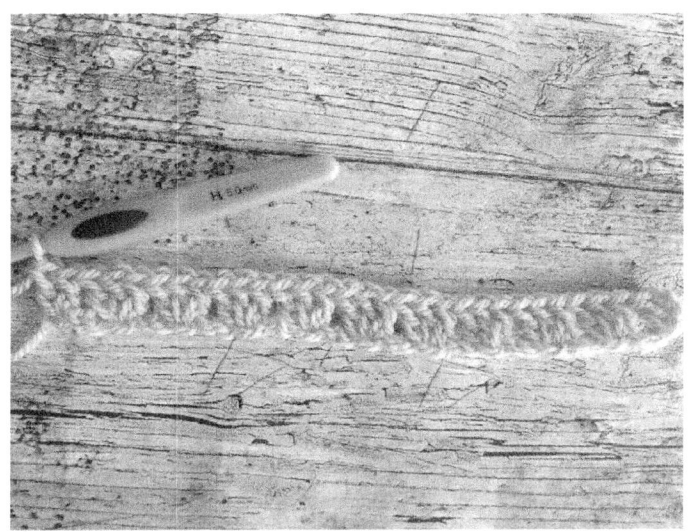

Row 2 chain 3, 3 dc in the next sp (in between the first 2 dc and the next 3 dc) and in each sp along the row. End with 1 dc in the last stitch (top of chain 3 from previous row). Turn.

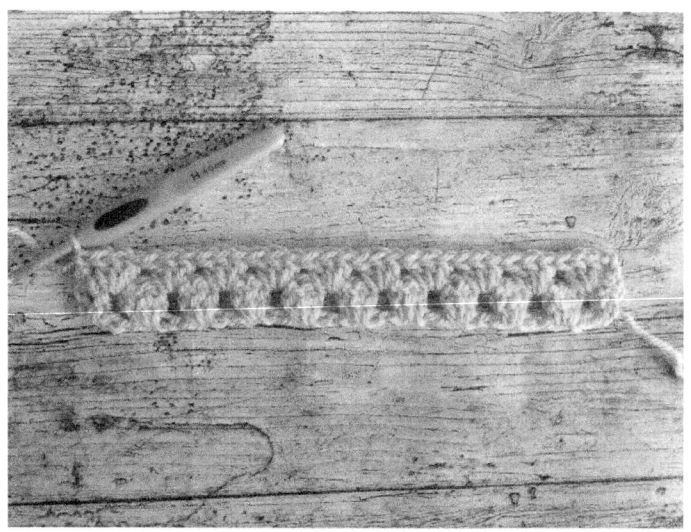

Row 3 chain 3, dc in the first sp, 3 dc in the next space and every space along finishing with 2 dc in the last sp. Turn

Rows 2 and 3 form the pattern, continue in this way changing colours when ever you like...

How To Crochet Blanket

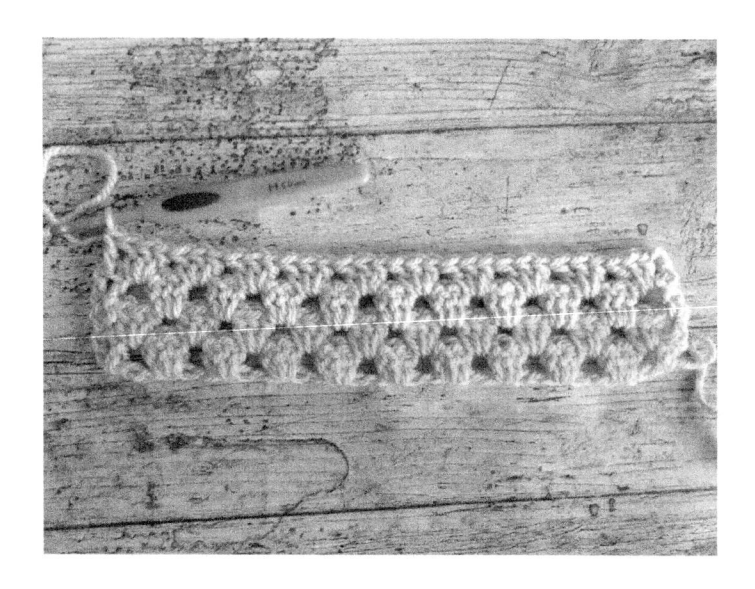

...until your blanket is the desired length. Fasten off and weave in ends.

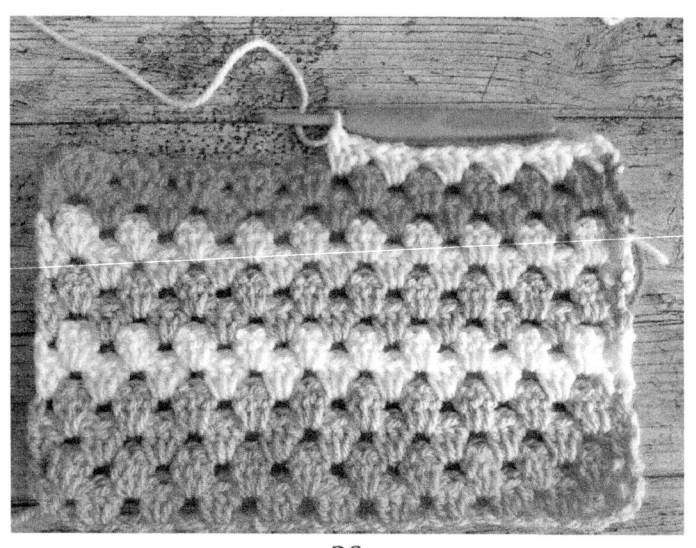

You could end up with something like this...

Twinkling Stars Blanket

How To Crochet Blanket

Materials

1. Worsted Weight yarn which is on the thinner side. I used Caron Simply Soft in colors Strawberry, Robins egg and White.

2. Hook H (5mm). If you crochet loose, you might want to go down to 4.5mm hook.

3. Tapestry needle to weave in the ends.

Finished Size

38 1/2 inches wide and 38 1/2 inches long.

Yardage

1 skein of the blue and white color and 2 skeins of the pink as it is used for the border as well. Each skein is 315 yards or 170g.

Stitch Abbreviations

beg- beginning

sk- skip

ch- chain

sc- single crochet

dc- double crochet

hdc- half double crochet

st- stitch

ch-loop- chain loop

Stitch Explanations

Shell: 5 dc worked into the same st.

Gauge

How To Crochet Blanket

15 dc sts = 4 inches

With pink color yarn, Ch 164. You can chain any multiple of 16+20 if you want to make your blanket smaller or bigger.

Row 1 completed

Row 1: 2 dc in 4th ch from hook, sk 2 chs, sc in next, ch 1, sk 1, sc in next st, *(sk 2 chs, shell in next st, sk 2 chs, 1 sc in next, ch 1, sk 1, sc in next), repeat

from * to last 3 chs, sk 2 chs, 3 dc in last ch. Turn.
——19 shells+ 2 half shells

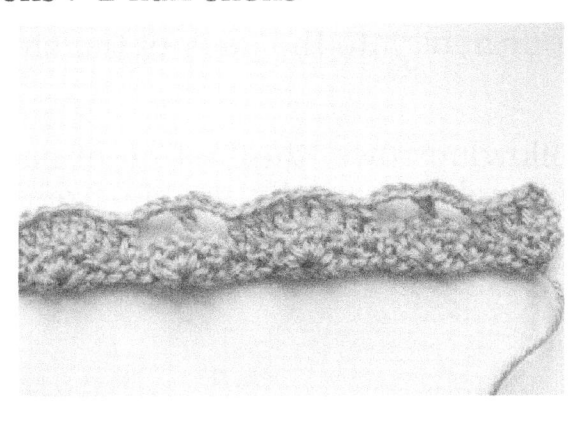

Row 2 completed

Row 2: Ch 3 (counts as a dc here and throughout), 1 dc in next 2 dc, 1 dc in next sc, 1 dc in next ch-1 space between the sc sts, ch 3, sk next sc and 2 dc, 1 dc in next dc in the middle of the shell, ch 3, sk 3 sts, 1 dc in next ch-1 space between sc sts, 1 dc in next sc, *(1 dc in next 5 dc of the shell, 1 dc in next sc, 1 dc in next ch-1 space, ch 3, sk 3 sts, 1 dc in next dc in the middle of the shell, ch 3, sk 3 sts, 1 dc in next ch-1 space, 1 dc in next sc), repeat from * to last 3 sts, 1 dc in next 2 sts, 1 dc on top of beginning ch-3. Turn.——101 dc

Notes

1. When you work sts into the chs, you will be inserting your hook into the back of the ch loops.

2. In the following rows, the first ch of each ch-loop will be squished and hardly visible from the back. Take care not to miss that.

Row 3 completed

Row 3: Ch 1 (not counted as a st here and throughout), 1 sc in the same st as beg ch-1, 1 sc in next dc, ch 5, *(sk 3 dc and 2 chs, 1 sc in next ch, ch 1, sk 1 dc, 1 sc in next ch, ch 5, sk 2 chs and next 3 dc, 1 sc in next dc**, ch 1, sk 1 dc, 1 sc in next dc, ch 5), repeat from * and end your last repeat at ** when just the beg ch-3 is left, 1 sc on top of beg ch-

3. Turn.——-20 ch-5 loops

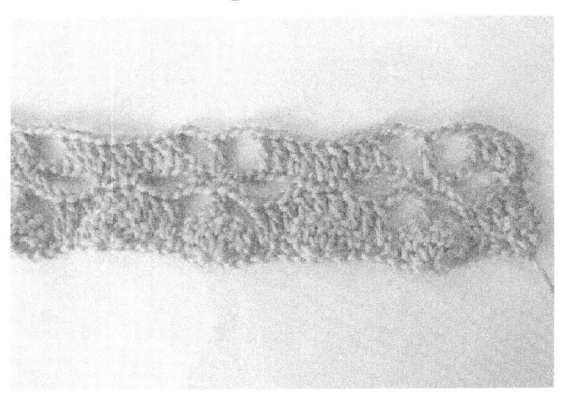

Row 4 completed

Row 4: Ch 3, 1 dc in next sc, 1 dc in next 3 chs, ch 3, sk next 2 chs and 1 sc, 1 dc in next ch-1 space between sc sts, *(ch 3, sk next sc and 2 chs, 1 dc in next 3 chs, 1 dc in next sc, 1 dc in next ch-1 space, 1 dc in next sc, 1 dc in next 3 chs, now you have 9 dc sts worked in a row, ch 3, sk 2 chs and 1 sc, 1 dc in next ch-1 space), repeat from * until you work a dc in the last ch-1 space and only one ch-5 loop is left, ch 3, sk next sc and 2 chs, 1 dc in last 3 chs and last 2 sc. Turn.——101 dc

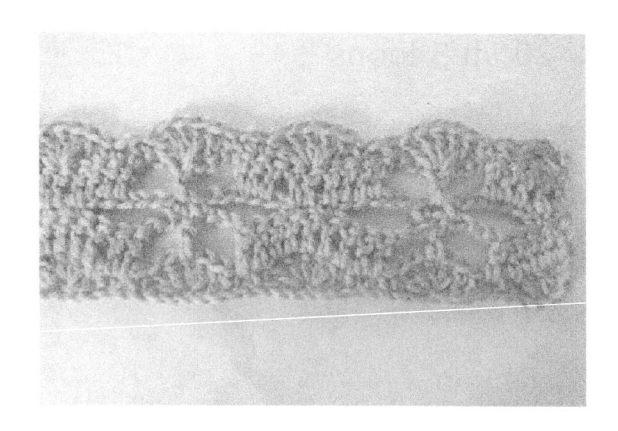

Row 5 completed

Row 5: Ch 3, 2 dc in the same st as beg ch-3, sk 2 dc, 1 sc in next, ch 1, sk 1 dc, 1 sc in next ch, *(sk 2 chs, shell on top of next dc, sk 2 chs, 1 sc in next ch, ch 1, sk 1 dc, 1 sc in next dc**, sk 2 dc, shell in next dc, sk 2 dc, 1 sc in next dc, ch 1, sk 1 dc, 1 sc in next ch), repeat from * and end last repeat at ** when you have 3 sts left, sk next 2 dc, 3 dc on top of beg ch-3, join white color yarn. Turn. ——-19 shells + 2 half shells

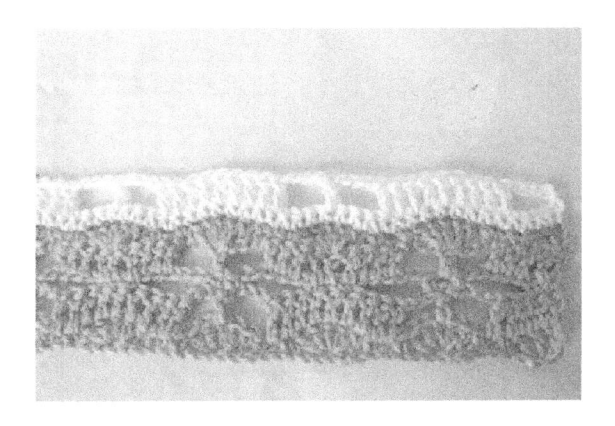

Row 6 and 7 worked in white

Row 6: Ch 1, 1 sc in the same st as beg ch-1, 1 sc in each st and ch-1 space across to end. Turn.—-161 sc

Row 7: Ch 6, sk next 3 sts, 1 dc in next 9 sts, *(ch 3, sk next 3 sts, 1 dc in next st, ch 3, sk next 3 sts, 1 dc in next 9 sts), repeat from * to last 4 sts, ch 3, sk 3 sts, 1 dc on top of last sc. Turn.——-101 dc

Row 8 completed

Row 8: Ch 1, 1 sc in same st as ch 1, 1 sc in next ch, *(ch 5, sk 2 chs and next 3 dc, 1 sc in next dc, ch 1, sk 1, 1 sc in next dc**, ch 5, sk 3 dc and 2 chs, 1 sc in next ch, ch 1, sk 1 dc, sc in next ch), repeat from * and end last repeat at **, ch 5, sk 3 dc and 2 chs, 1 sc in next 2 chs. Turn.————-20 ch-5 loops

Row 9 completed

Row 9: Ch 6, *(sk next sc and 2 chs, 1 dc in next 3 chs, 1 dc in next sc, 1 dc in next ch-1 space, 1 dc in next sc, 1 dc in next 3 chs, now you have 9 sts worked in a row**, ch 3, sk next 2 chs and 1 sc, 1 dc in next ch-1 space, ch 3), repeat from * and end last repeat at **, ch 3, sk 2 chs and 1 sc, 1 dc in very last sc. Turn.——-101 dc

Row 10 completed

Row 10: Ch 3, 2 dc in same st as ch 3, sk 2 chs, 1 sc in next ch, ch 1, sk 1 dc, 1 sc in next dc, *(sk 2 dc, shell in next dc, sk 2 dc, 1 sc in next dc, ch 1, sk 1 dc, 1 sc in next ch**, sk 2 chs, 1 shell in next dc, sk 2 chs, 1 sc in next ch, ch 1, sk 1 dc, 1 sc in next dc), repeat from * and end last repeat at **, sk 2 chs, 3 dc on next ch. Join the blue color yarn. Turn.—-19 shells + 2 half shells

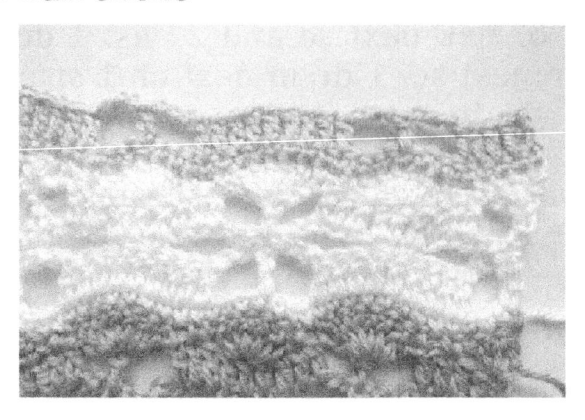

Row 11 and 12 worked in blue

Row 11: Ch 1, 1 sc in the same st as beg ch-1, 1 sc in each st and ch-1 space across to end. Turn.—-161 sc

Row 12: Ch 3, 1 dc in next 4 sts, ch 3, sk 3 sts, 1 dc in next, *(ch 3, sk 3 sts, 1 dc in next 9 sts, ch 3, sk 3 sts, 1 dc in next), repeat from * to last 8 sts, ch 3, sk 3 sts, 1 dc in last 5 sts. Turn. —-101 dc

Repeat Rows 3-12 for the pattern and end with Row 10 in pink color, do not fasten off and do not turn.

How To Crochet Blanket

Take care to follow the color sequence you want for your blanket by changing colors at the end of Rows 5 and 10.

Pom Pom Border for Your Crochet Blanket

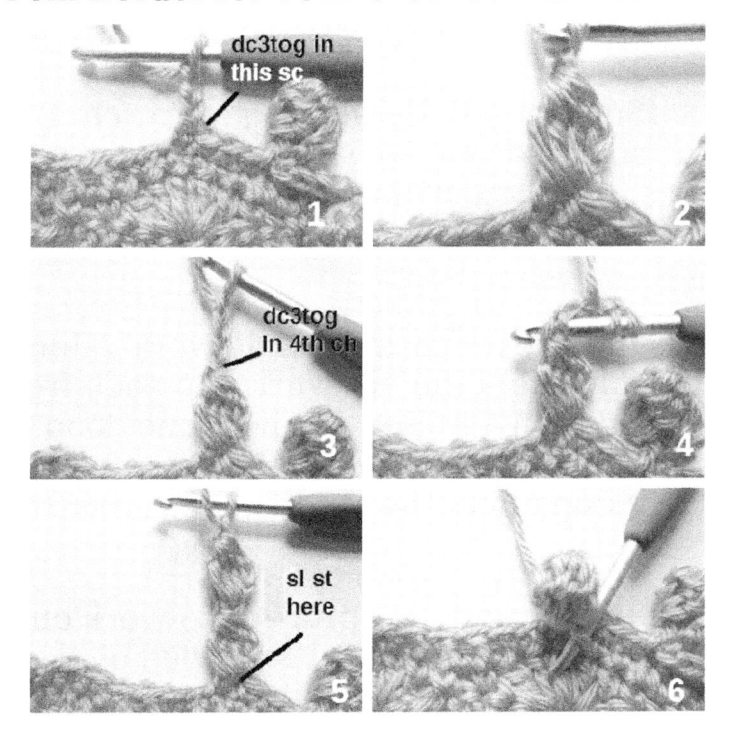

Notes

1. You will first work a round of sc around the blanket without turning your work.

2. This is included at the end showing you how to make the pom pom border.

Round 1 (Sc Row): With working yarn, ch 1 at the corner, 3 sc in corner, working along the edges of the stripes, evenly distribute sc. I worked around 8 sc across the end of each stripe.

3 sc at the next corner and work along the foundation ch side. I did not work into each free loop of the foundation ch but skipped one loop under each shell to get approximately 145 sts, 3 sc in next corner, work up along the stripe edges again.

3 sc in the corner and now proceed to work on top of your last row to level it out. 1 sc in beg ch-3, 1 sc in next 2 dc sts, 1 sc in next sc, 1 sc in next ch-1 space, 1 hdc in next st, *(1 sc in next 2 dc of shell, sk next st on peak, 1 sc in last 2 dc of shell, 1 sc in next sc, 1 sc in next ch-1 space, 1 hdc in next st), repeat from * to last 3 sts, 1 sc in last 3 sts, sl st to the first sc in corner. Do not turn.

Notes

1. Along the edges of the stripes, I added one pom pom at the junction of 2 stripes and one at the middle of each stripe.

2. On the foundation ch side and the last row side, you have 4 sc between pom poms but you can adjust that number to suit your stitch count. In case you have only 4 sts left to the corner, work 3 sc instead of 4 and so on.

Stitch Explanation

Pom Pom: 1 sc in the specified st, ch 3, 1 dc3tog in the sc you just worked to make the first half of your pom pom, ch 1 to close, ch 4, dc3tog into the 4th ch from hook, take care to catch one extra loop behind the ch, close the top half over the bottom half and sl st to the sc at the very base of the pom pom.

Round 2 (Pom Pom Round): Ch 1, 1 pom pom in next st, *(1 sc in each st to reach the middle of a stripe, pop pom in the next st, 1 sc in each st to reach the junction of 2 stripes, pom pom in the junction), repeat from * to end of the side.

1 sc in corner, 1 pom pom in the same st, 1 more sc in the same corner st, *(1 sc in next 4 sts, 1 pom pom in the next st), repeat from * to end of this side.

1 sc in corner st, 1 pom pom in same corner st, 1 more sc in the corner st, work along the edges of stripes working a pom pom at the middle and end of each stripe like before.

1 sc in corner, 1 pom pom in the same st, 1 more sc in the same corner st, *(1 sc in next 4 sts, 1 pom pom in the next st), repeat from * to end of this side. Sl st to the base of the first pop pom and fasten off.

Printed in Great Britain
by Amazon